From
the Library
of

of

Ray Bripner

B213 © APCo

LET'S EAT OUT
How to read menus in Japanese

LET'S EAT OUT

How to read menus in Japanese

by Philip J. Hinder

The Japan Times

ISBN4-7890-0408-2

First edition: June 1988

Illustrations by Masako Bando
Jacket design and Layout by CADEC, Inc.

Published by The Japan Times, Ltd.
5-4, Shibaura 4-chome, Minato-ku, Tokyo 108, Japan

Printed in Japan

For
Trevor-San

CONTENTS

7

ACKNOWLEDGEMENTS

I would like to thank all friends and colleagues in Japan for their encouragement and help, and the people of Tokyo for making the "research" for this book such an enjoyable experience.

I'd especially like to express my gratitude to Ms. Masako Bando for doing the illustrations and offering her professional advice.

I

INTRODUCTION

Learning to read Japanese is not something that can be done in a short time and without a lot of effort, and so the Japanese syllabaries (*Hiragana* and *Katakana*) and *Kanji* (originally derived from Chinese) might at first seem daunting. There are a number of books currently available for the student of Japanese that break down the myth that the language is too difficult for the English native speaker to master. However, an immediate problem for the visitor to Japan, and also for the resident who may not have had the time or the opportunity to study much Japanese, is **how to order food and drink in ordinary restaurants and bars that do not have a menu written in English.** Even the more serious student will find it takes time to master the reading of menus since the vocabulary is specialized and the *Kanji* regularly found are not necessarily those considered the most important in the field of study.

This book concentrates on the written language needed to be understood in most kinds of restaurants, snack bars and drinking places in Japan. It is of use to the short-term visitor but it is especially geared to the needs of the longer-term resident. In addition to being a handy reference book, it may also be regarded as a practical introduction to the Japanese language. It is arranged in order of difficulty and the language presented is immediately usable. **No previous knowledge of Japanese is required** and, besides the extensive sample menus, useful conversational phrases are included in addition to other relevant information about the various kinds of food and restaurants.

JAPANESE SYLLABARY ('KATAKANA')

There are two sets of *Kana*—*Hiragana* and *Katakana*—each consisting of 45 basic symbols. The sounds in each system are identical but, as a rule, *Katakana* is used for special emphasis and to write 'borrowed' foreign words which are usually refined or abbreviated and therefore might sound rather different from the original word.

Normal written Japanese is made up of *Kanji* with the *Hiragana* supplying the grammatical endings etc. with a few *Katakana* words included. However, any Japanese word can be written entirely in *Hiragana* instead of using *Kanji* and sometimes there is no *Kanji* equivalent.

Most *Kana* symbols represent one syllable, consisting of a consonant followed by a vowel. Also, the five vowels are represented on their own and the *N* sound completes the list. Up to Chapter VI of this book, the establishments examined have menus mainly written in *Katakana* and so it's easiest to start with the *Katakana* chart:

ア	カ	サ	タ	ナ	ハ	マ	ヤ	ラ	ワ	ン
a	ka	sa	ta	na	ha	ma	ya	ra	wa	n
イ	キ	シ	チ	ニ	ヒ	ミ		リ		
i	ki	shi	chi	ni	hi	mi		ri		
ウ	ク	ス	ツ	ヌ	フ	ム	ユ	ル		
u	ku	su	tsu	nu	fu	mu	yu	ru		
エ	ケ	セ	テ	ネ	ヘ	メ		レ		
e	ke	se	te	ne	he	me		re		
オ	コ	ソ	ト	ノ	ホ	モ	ヨ	ロ		
o	ko	so	to	no	ho	mo	yo	ro		

Each syllable is of equal length and unstressed. The vowel sounds are approximately as follows, but are shorter than their English equivalents:

a as in 'rather'
i as in 'been'
u as in 'blue'
e as in 'met'
o as in 'hot'

Other sounds are formed by adding two small lines ＼ (*Dakuten*) or a small circle ° (*Han-dakuten*) to certain *Kana*.

For example:

	カ	キ	ク	ケ	コ
	ka	*ki*	*ku*	*ke*	*ko*
becomes					
	ガ	ギ	グ	ゲ	ゴ
	ga	*gi*	*gu*	*ge*	*go*

Adding ˮ to the S-line forms the Z-line: *za, ji, zu, ze, zo.*
Adding ˮ to the T-line forms the D-line: *da, ji, zu, de, do.*
Adding ˮ to the H-line forms the B-line: *ba, bi, bu, be, bo.*
Adding ° to the H-line forms the P-line: *pa, pi, pu, pe, po.*

The above rules are true for both *Katakana* and *Hiragana*. A straight line is used to double the length of the vowel sound in *Katakana* only. For example, コ— is pronounced *Kō*. In the following chapters, a line above a vowel lengthens it, although for clarity, a long *i* is written *ii*.

Kana may be combined to form one syllable:

	キャ	チュ	ニョ	
	kya	*chu*	*nyo*	,etc.

Note that the second *Kana* is smaller in this case. A small ツ (*Tsu*) is not pronounced but doubles the consonant which follows it. In practice, slightly hesitating before the consonant and stressing it produces the right effect.

Lastly, an *N* before a 'B', 'P' or 'M' sounds as an 'M' and therefore will be written as an *M*.

III

IN A CAFÉ

喫茶店

コーヒー店

There are cafés everywhere in Japan and some cater for individual tastes with jazz or classical music, for example. They are generally clean and comfortable and customers stay for a long time over one cup of coffee. The price of a drink is not cheap when compared to other countries although breakfast or lunch 'sets' are good value.

Menus in cafés are almost completely in *Katakana* since many 'foreign' words are included. However, it is important to pronounce the words as if they are 'Japanese,' without undue stress and with syllables of equal length.

Most items you are likely to come across are listed below and each café will have only a limited selection. The second column is written in *Rōmaji* (as you should say it) and the third column gives the English 'translation.' Practice saying each word aloud and, when you can remember some *Katakana*, try testing yourself by covering up the second and third columns. Sometimes you can guess the symbols you have forgotten once you recognize the word. A few common *Kanji* are also introduced.

●——DRINKS　　ドリンク [Dorinku]

コーヒー（珈琲）	*Kōhii*	Coffee
ブレンドコーヒー	*Burendo Kōhii*	Blend Coffee
アメリカンコーヒー	*Amerikan Kōhii*	American Coffee
ウインナコーヒー	*Uinna Kōhii*	Viennese Coffee
アイスコーヒー	*Aisu Kōhii*	Iced Coffee
カフェオーレ	*Kafe Ōre*	Café Au Lait
エスプレッソ	*Esupuresso*	Café Espresso
モ　カ	*Moka*	Mocha Coffee
コロンビア	*Korombia*	Colombian Coffee
キリマンジャロ	*Kirimanjaro*	Kilimanjaro Coffee
ブルーマウンテン	*Burū Maunten*	Blue Mountain Coffee
紅茶	*Kōcha*	Tea (Black)
レモンティー	*Remon Tii*	Tea With Lemon
ミルクティー	*Miruku Tii*	Tea With Milk
アイスティー	*Aisu Tii*	Iced Tea
ミルク	*Miruku*	Milk
ココア	*Kokoa*	Cocoa
コーラ	*Kōra*	Cola
コーラフロート	*Kōra Furōto*	Cola Float
オレンジジュース	*Orenji Jūsu*	Orange Juice
トマトジュース	*Tomato Jūsu*	Tomato Juice
リンゴジュース	*Ringo Jūsu*	Apple Juice
レモンスカッシュ	*Remon Sukasshu*	Lemon Squash
メロンソーダ	*Meron Sōda*	Melon Soda (With Ice Cream)
クリームソーダ	*Kuriimu Sōda*	Cream Soda (A Green Soda With Ice Cream)
ビール	*Biiru*	Beer

●──FOOD　　　　　食　物 [Tabemono]

サンド	Sando	Sandwich
サンドイッチ	Sandoitchi	Sandwich
ハムサンド	Hamu Sando	Ham Sandwich
ツナサンド	Tsuna Sando	Tuna Sandwich
玉子サンド	Tamago Sando	Egg Sandwich
野菜サンド	Yasai Sando	Salad Sandwich
ミックスサンド	Mikkusu Sando	Mixed Sandwich
バタートースト	Batā Tōsuto	Buttered Toast
ジャムトースト	Jamu Tōsuto	Toast With Jam
チーズトースト	Chiizu Tōsuto	Cheese On Toast
ピザトースト	Piza Tōsuto	Pizza-style Toast
クロワッサン	Kurowassan	Croissant
スパゲティ	Supagetii	Spaghetti
ナポリタン	Naporitan	Spaghetti Napolitana
ミートソース	Miito Sōsu	Spaghetti Bolognese
和風スパゲティ	Wafū Supagetii	Japanese-style Spaghetti
カレーライス	Karē Raisu	Yellow Curry (Mild) With Rice
ドライカレー	Dorai Karē	Dry Curry With Rice
ピラフ	Pirafu	Pilaf
カニピラフ	Kani Pirafu	Crab Pilaf
エビピラフ	Ebi Pirafu	Shrimp Pilaf
オムライス	Omuraisu	Rice Omelette (With Small Pieces Of Chiken And Tomato Ketchup)

●──DESSERTS　　デザート [Dezāto]

アイスクリーム	*Aisu Kuriimu*	Ice Cream
ケーキ	*Kēki*	Cake
ホットケーキ	*Hotto Kēki*	Hot Cake
チーズケーキ	*Chiizu Kēki*	Cheesecake
チョコレートケーキ	*Chokorēto Kēki*	Chocolate Cake
ゼリー	*Zerii*	Jelly
コーヒーゼリー	*Kōhii Zerii*	Coffee-flavored Jelly
チョコレートパフェ	*Chokorēto Pafe*	Chocolate Sundae ('Parfait')
バナナパフェ	*Banana Pafe*	Banana Sundae
プリン	*Purin*	'Pudding' (Crème Caramel)
フルーツクレープ	*Furūtsu Kurēpu*	Fruit Pancake ('Crêpe')

▶▶ VOCABULARY ·······················

紅　茶 [*Kōcha*] This is *BLACK TEA* as opposed to Japanese Green Tea. It is generally served with lemon unless you ask for milk.

野　菜 [*Yasai*] *VEGETABLES*. This often means just 'Salad'.

和　風 [*Wafū*] *JAPANESE-STYLE*. *Wafū Supagetii* includes seaweed and mushrooms and is flavored with soy sauce.

●●● USEFUL LANGUAGE ·······················

★ When you walk in, you'll be greeted with *Irasshaimase*.

★ If you need a menu, you should say, *Menyū o misete kudasai* (*lit.* Please show me the menu).

★ Order like this: *Kōhii o kudasai* or *Kōhii onegaishimasu*.

.....*o kudasai* means 'Please give me.....' whereas *Onegaishimasu* has the meaning of 'Please do it for me.'

★ If you want to order two coffees, say *Kōhii o futatsu kudasai.*

★ 'Yes' and 'No' in Japanese are *Hai* and *Iie* respectively.

★ When you want to find the toilet, say *Toire wa doko desu ka?*, and when you'd like some water, ask for *Omizu o kudasai.*

★ Finally, *Arigatō* means 'Thank you' and *Sayōnara* 'Goodbye.'

NOTE

Before about 11 a.m., look out for 'Morning Service' (モーニングサービス *Mōningu Sābisu*) which generally includes toast, a boiled egg, a small salad and a choice of tea or coffee. When the waiter or waitress asks *Nomimono wa?* ('What would you like to drink?'), ask for *Hotto Kōhii*, *Aisu Kōhii*, or *Kōcha*. Between 12 and 2 p.m., there may be a special lunch ランチ (*Ranchi*) and some places offer a 'Cake Set' ケーキセット (*Kēki Setto*) which works out cheaper than ordering the items separately. The *Kanji* 付 (*Tsuki*) indicates that a drink, for example, is included in the price: コーヒー又はティー付 (= 'Coffee or tea is included').

Numbers in Japanese

Numbers 1-10 are as follows:

1	*Hitotsu*	一		**6**	*Muttsu*	六
2	*Futatsu*	二		**7**	*Nanatsu*	七
3	*Mittsu*	三		**8**	*Yattsu*	八
4	*Yottsu*	四		**9**	*Kokonotsu*	九
5	*Itsutsu*	五		**10**	*Tō*	十

IN A KOREAN-STYLE 'YAKINIKU' RESTAURANT

焼 肉

Yakiniku restaurants, often called 'Korean Barbecue' restaurants, are very popular in Japan and can be easily recognized by a sign with the distinctive *Kanji* 焼 肉 prominently displayed outside. *Yakiniku* may be translated as 'Cooked Meat' and you grill the meat and vegetables in front of you at the table. The meat is then dipped into a spicy sauce before being eaten. Again the menu is mainly in *Katakana* as the names of the dishes were not originally Japanese. The most popular items are written here and this menu is pretty standard in the majority of restaurants of this type.

●—MEAT etc.

ロース	*Rōsu*	Tender Slices (Of Beef)
上ロース	*Jō Rōsu*	Best *Rōsu*

カルビ	*Karubi*	A Cheaper Cut Of Meat (With Fat)
タン〔舌〕	*Tan*	Tongue
ミ ノ	*Mino*	Tripe (Part Of Stomach)
ユッケ	*Yukke*	Minced Meat With Egg Yolk
ハツ焼	*Hatsu Yaki*	Heart
レバー焼	*Rebā Yaki*	Liver
イカ焼	*Ika Yaki*	Squid
生野菜焼	*Namayasai Yaki*	Fresh Vegetables

●—OTHER DISHES

ユッケ刺	*Yukke Sashi*	Raw Minced Meat With Egg Yolk
レバー刺	*Rebā Sashi*	Raw Liver
イカ刺	*Ika Sashi*	Raw Squid
カクテキ	*Kakuteki*	Pickled Radish
ナムル	*Namuru*	Spinach, Bean Sprouts, Radish, etc.
キムチ	*Kimuchi*	'Kim Chee.' Pickled White Cabbage (Spicy)
オイキムチ	*Oi Kimuchi*	Pickled Cucumber
ライス	*Raisu*	Rice

●—SOUP　　　　スープ [*Sūpu*]

玉子スープ	*Tamago Sūpu*	Egg Soup
ワカメスープ	*Wakame Sūpu*	Seaweed Soup
テグタンスープ	*Tegutan Sūpu*	Spicy Soup
クッパ	*Kuppa*	Spicy Soup With Meat And Vegetables

| ビビンバ | *Bibimba* | Soup With 'Namuru' And Boiled Rice |

●—SET MEALS   定 食 [*Teishoku*]

| 焼肉弁当 | *Yakiniku Bentō* | *Yakiniku* Lunch |
| 焼肉定食 | *Yakiniku Teishoku* | *Yakiniku* Set Meal |

●—DRINKS   飲み物 [*Nomimono*]

ビール	*Biiru*	Beer
生ビール	*Nama Biiru*	Draught Beer
お 酒	*Osake*	Sake

"It must be nearly done ...."

▶▶ VOCABULARY ·····················

焼 [Yaki] This generally means *GRILLED* but may also be translated as 'Broiled' (for fish) and 'Baked' (for bread) amongst other things.

肉 [Niku] *MEAT*. In 'Korean Barbecue' restaurants, beef 牛肉 (*Gyūniku*) is used. For future reference, the *Kanji* for pork (*Butaniku*) is 豚肉 and for chicken (*Toriniku*) it is 鳥肉.

生 [Nama] *Nama Yasai* means *RAW* or *FRESH* vegetables, whereas *Nama Biiru* is often translated as *DRAUGHT* (or even 'Live!') beer, although it is also available in bottles.

刺 [Sashi] *SLICES OF RAW MEAT, etc.* The same *Kanji* is also used for *Sashimi* (刺身 'Raw Fish') - see Chapter X.

弁 当 [Bentō] *BOXED LUNCH*. Yakiniku restaurants sometimes serve lunch in this style, with meat, *Kimuchi* and rice in separate compartments. Many Japanese people bring their *Bentō* from home every day or buy them at the station (called *Eki Ben*).

定 食 [Teishoku] *SET MEAL*. This is a good value, all-inclusive meal with rice, soup, pickles and a drink. In some places, *Teishoku* may only be available at lunchtimes.

お 酒 [Osake] *SAKE*. This 'Rice Wine' may be served hot (ask for *Atsukan*) and comes in a *Tokkuri* (special jar). The *O* in *Osake* makes it more polite and it is customary for many words to be preceded by *O*.

★ *Konnichiwa* is 'Hello' and *Kombanwa* 'Good Evening.'

★ To attract the waiter's attention, call out *Sumimasen* (Excuse me).

★ Before eating, it is customary to say *Itadakimasu*.

★ To order two portions of *Rōsu*, you can say, *Rōsu o futatsu kudasai* or *Rōsu o ni-ninmae kudasai*.
  -ninmae means 'Portion' and the prefix *ni* in the example means 'Two.'

★ Before drinking, say *Kampai!* (Cheers!).

★ When you have finished your meal, or when you are leaving the restaurant, it is polite to say *Gochisōsama deshita* (*lit.* Thank you for your delicious food).

Numbers in Japanese

The prefixes for the numbers 1-10 (and which are also the cardinal numbers) are:

1	*Ichi*	一	**6**	*Roku*	六
2	*Ni*	二	**7**	*Nana*	七
3	*San*	三	**8**	*Hachi*	八
4	*Yon*	四	**9**	*Kyū*	九
5	*Go*	五	**10**	*Jū*	十

The counter for long, thin objects is *-hon* and so we can use this to order bottles of beer, for example. Notice that *hon* becomes *bon* and *pon* in some cases and some forms are contracted:

Ippon (1 bottle)	一本	*Roppon* (6 bottles)	六本
Nihon (2 bottles)	二本	*Nanahon* (7 bottles)	七本
Sanbon (3 bottles)	三本	*Happon* (8 bottles)	八本
Yonhon (4 bottles)	四本	*Kyūhon* (9 bottles)	九本
Gohon (5 bottles)	五本	*Juppon* (10 bottles)	十本

Therefore, *Biiru o yonhon onegaishimasu* = 'Four bottles of beer please.'

Use the counter *-hai* for counting glasses (of drinks) like this: *Ippai, Nihai, Sanbai,* etc.

IN A 'WESTERN-STYLE' FAMILY RESTAURANT

ファミリーレストラン

These 'Family Restaurants' offer mainly Western-style cooking with a few popular Japanese dishes thrown in for good measure. Although many 'chain' restaurants have a standard menu, generally the menus vary considerably from place to place. Many items featured in Chapter III will be included and some additional *Katakana* words are written here. The more difficult items you are likely to come across will be covered later on.

●—MENU   メニュー [*Menyū*]

ミックスピザ	*Mikkusu Piza*	Mixed Pizza
グラタン	*Guratan*	Gratin (Macaroni Cheese)
オムレツ	*Omuretsu*	Omelette
ハンバーグステーキ	*Hambāgu Sutēki*	Hamburg Steak

ビーフシチュー	*Biifu Shichū*	Beef Stew
ビーフステーキ	*Biifu Sutēki*	Beefsteak
ビフテキ	*Bifuteki*	Beefsteak
サーロインステーキ	*Sāroin Sutēki*	Sirloin Steak
ポークジンジャー	*Pōku Jinjā*	Pork With Ginger
ポークしょうが焼	*Pōku Shōgayaki*	Pork With Ginger
チキンテリヤキ	*Chikin Teriyaki*	Chicken 'Teriyaki-style'
セット	*Setto*	Set Meal
パ　ン	*Pan*	Bread

▶▶ **VOCABULARY** ··································

テリヤキ	[*Teriyaki*] Meat or fish *COOKED IN A SWEET SAUCE.*
セット	[*Setto*] *SET MEAL.* Similar to *Teishoku* but with a choice of rice or bread and with a side salad and tea or coffee.
パ　ン	[*Pan*] *BREAD.* A soft, sweet roll and butter is served in most 'Family Restaurants.' Sometimes it is called *Rōru Pan.*

NOTE

Usually the breakfasts are more substantial here than the 'Mōningu Setto' offered in coffee shops and so you might be able to find Ham and Egg (ハムエッグ *Hamu Eggu*), or Bacon and Egg (ベーコンエッグ *Bēkon Eggu*). Although cafés serve boiled eggs (ゆで卵 *Yude Tamago*), 'Family Restaurants' are also likely to have fried egg (目玉焼 *Medama Yaki*) and scrambled egg (いり卵 *Iri Tamago*).

SOME OTHER FOREIGN FOOD RESTAURANTS

For extra practice, below are some examples of food available in restaurants serving Italian, German and Indian food.

●━ITALIAN FOOD　イタリア料理

エビピザ	*Ebi Piza*	Shrimp Pizza
スパゲティ・バジリコ	*Supagetii Bajiriko*	Spaghetti With Basil
スパゲティ・ボンゴレ	*Supagetii Bongore*	Spaghetti Vongole (With Clams)
カネロニ	*Kaneroni*	Cannelloni
パスタとシーフードのチーズ焼	*Pasuta to Shiifūdo no Chiizu Yaki*	Pasta And Seafood Grilled With Cheese
マカロニグラタン	*Makaroni Guratan*	Macaroni Cheese
シーフードドリア	*Shiifūdo Doria*	Seafood Doria (With Rice)
魚貝のマリネ	*Gyokai no Marine*	Seafood Mariné

⬤──GERMAN FOOD   ドイツ料理

アイスバイン	*Aisubain*	Knuckle of Pork ('Eisbein')
カスラーリペン	*Kasurāripen*	Smoked Pork Chop
ザワークラウト	*Zawākurauto*	'Saüerkraut'
ウインナ	*Uinna*	Wiener Sausage
フランクフルト	*Furankufuruto*	Frankfurter
クナックブルスト	*Kunakkuburusuto*	'Knackwurst'
ソーセージの盛合せ	*Sōsēji no Moriawase*	A Selection of Sausages

⬤──INDIAN FOOD   インド料理

ビーフカレー	*Biifu Karē*	Beef Curry
チキンカレー	*Chikin Karē*	Chicken Curry
マトンカレー	*Maton Karē*	Mutton Curry
野菜カレー	*Yasai Karē*	Vegetable Curry
サーグチキン	*Sāgu Chikin*	Chicken With Spinach ('Sag Chicken')
タンドリーチキン	*Tandorii Chikin*	Tandori Chicken
マトンティカ	*Maton Tika*	'Mutton Tikka'
ナ　ン	*Nan*	Nan (Bread)

★ Note that, although tipping is unnecessary in restaurants, 10% is added to your bill when the amount exceeds a certain amount per person (currently ¥2,500) and some of the more expensive establishments levy an additional service charge.

★ If you want to know if a particular thing is available, you can use the phrase ......*wa arimasu ka?*. Thus, *Aisu Kuriimu wa arimasu ka?* means 'Do you have any ice cream?'

★ When you have eaten enough, *Mō kekkō desu* (No more, thank you) is appropriate and to ask for the bill, say either *Ikura desu ka?* (How much is it?) or *Okanjō o onegaishimasu* (Please bring the bill). If you need a receipt, the word is *Ryōshūsho*.

Numbers in Japanese

The cardinal numbers listed in Chapter IV are also used for counting money. *Yen* (pronounced *en*) may be written as ¥ preceding the amount or as えん or 円 following the number. Other important numbers are:

100	*Hyaku*	百
1,000	*Sen*	千
10,000	*(Ichi-)Man*	(一)万

Therefore, *Sen ni-hyaku go-jū en* = ¥1,250
Similarly, *Hassen roppyaku jū-go en* = ¥8,615
and *San-man nana-sen san-byaku hachi-jū en* = ¥37,380.

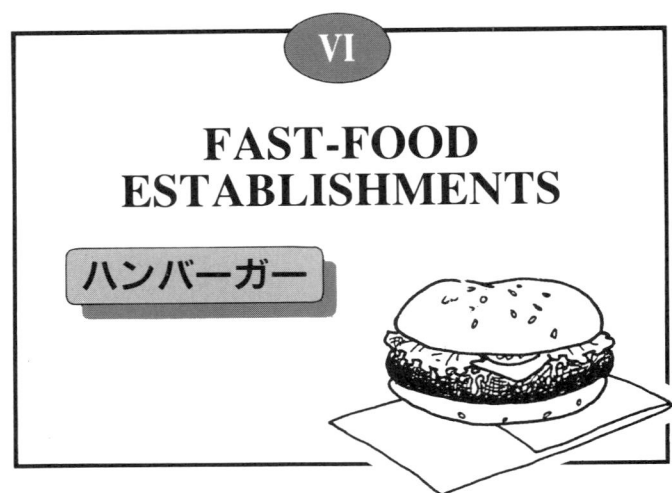

VI

FAST-FOOD ESTABLISHMENTS

ハンバーガー

As is readily apparent, hamburger joints and other fast-food outlets are in abundance everywhere and the big American chains are represented, in addition to numerous Japanese versions. Besides the usual hamburgers, fish and chicken, desserts and soft drinks, many offer a selection of ice cream etc. The surroundings are typically bland although hordes of students flock to these places after school. Their popularity is guaranteed in a society which is always on the move and they provide an alternative to the noodle-stands where company workers grab a quick bite between trains.

The basically American import is adapted, though, to cater for the Japanese market, so don't be surprised to find 'Teriyaki Burgers' or 'Octopus Salad' (*Tako Sarada*) on the menu. Everything is written in *Katakana* and even words like 'Large' (*Rāji*) and 'Small' (*Sumōru*)—or 'L' and 'S'—are used instead of the original Japanese words.

However, as it can sometimes be more difficult to make yourself understood when using 'foreign' words than when using 'Japanese' ones, it cannot be emphasized enough that your pronunciation must be consistent with the *Katakana* system.

This menu incorporates most of the items commonly found in the major fast-food chains:

●—BURGERS　　　バーガー [*Bāgā*]

ハンバーガー	*Hambāgā*	Hamburger
チーズバーガー	*Chiizu Bāgā*	Cheeseburger
チーズハンバーガー	*Chiizu Hambāgā*	Cheeseburger
フィッシュバーガー	*Fisshu Bāgā*	Fishburger
チキンバーガー	*Chikin Bāgā*	Chickenburger
エビバーガー	*Ebi Bāgā*	Shrimpburger
テリヤキバーガー	*Teriyaki Bāgā*	'Teriyaki' burger
テリヤキビーフバーガー	*Teriyaki Biifu Bāgā*	'Teriyaki' burger

●—OTHER FOOD

チキンナゲット	*Chikin Nagetto*	Chicken Nuggets
フライドチキン	*Furaido Chikin*	Fried Chicken
フライドポテト	*Furaido Poteto*	French-fried Potatoes

●—DRINKS　　　ドリンク [*Dorinku*]

コーヒー	*Kōhii*	Coffee
ミルク	*Miruku*	Milk
ジュース	*Jūsu*	Juice (=Soft Drink)

オレンジジュース	*Orenji Jūsu*	Orange Juice
スプライト	*Supuraito*	'Sprite'
コーラ	*Kōra*	Cola
シェイク	*Sheiku*	Milk Shake
バニラ	*Banira*	Vanilla
ストロベリー	*Sutoroberii*	Strawberry
チョコレート	*Chokorēto*	Chocolate
ヨーグルト	*Yōguruto*	Yoghurt

Note that other drinks, desserts, cakes, etc., may be found in Chapter III. Also, names of such items as 'Big Mac' and 'Filet o' fish' are transformed directly into *Katakana* as *Biggu Makku* and *Fire O Fisshu* and so on.

●●● USEFUL LANGUAGE ·····················

★ You'll be asked if your order is to 'eat here' (*Kochira de omeshiagari desu ka?*). You can say either, *Hai. Koko de tabemasu.* (I'll eat here) or *Mochikaeri* (To take away). The easier *Teiku auto* (Take out) is also widely used.

★ When ordering, the numbers *hitotsu, futatsu,* etc., may be used although it's often clearer to use *ikko, niko, sanko*....The suffix *-ko* can be used when counting objects.

★ When you have a choice of toppings, the words *iri* (with) and *nashi* (without) come after the word as follows:

    Hambāgā tomato nashi

(Hamburger without tomato)

    Chiizubāgā tomato iri

(Cheeseburger with tomato).

★ If you are asked *Nomimono wa ikaga desu ka?* (Would you like a drink?), or *Yoroshii desu ka?* (Is that all?), you can answer with *Kekkō desu* (That's all).

Numbers in Japanese

The tables are often on the second floor and so the assistant might say, *Nikai e dōzo* (Please go up to the second floor). The suffix *-kai* is used for the floors of a building, like this:

一階	*Ikkai*	1st Floor
二階	*Nikai*	2nd Floor
三階	*Sank[g]ai*	3rd Floor

Note that the floors are numbered as in the U.S.A. and also that the basement floors (often two or even three) are:

| B1 (1st Basement) | *Chika-ikkai* |
| B2 (2nd Basement) | *Chika-nikai* |

Chika means 'Underground' and is the same word as in *Chika tetsu* or 'Underground railway'.

TAKE-AWAY SHOPS

サンドイッチ

おべんとう

It is also worth mentioning the small, take-away shops which offer a variety of sandwiches, boxed lunches (*Bentō*) and sometimes rice balls and *Temaki* (a kind of *Sushi* — see Chapter X). Many foreigners consider the typically Japanese varieties more appetizing than the sandwiches with processed ham, curry croquette or even mandarin oranges and cream!

●──SANDWICHES サンドイッチ [*Sandoitchi*]

チーズサンド	*Chiizu Sando*	Cheese Sandwich
ハムサンド	*Hamu Sando*	Ham Sandwich
コロッケサンド	*Korokke Sando*	Curry Croquette Sandwich
フルーツサンド	*Furūtsu Sando*	Fruit Sandwich (see above)

カツサンド	*Katsu Sando*	Pork Cutlet Sandwich
ヤサイ（野菜）サンド	*Yasai Sando*	Salad Sandwich
タマゴ（玉子）サンド	*Tamago Sando*	Egg Sandwich

●——BOXED LUNCHES 弁 当 [Bentō]

牛弁当	*Gyū Bentō*	With Beef
焼肉弁当	*Yakiniku Bentō*	With Beef Or Pork
幕之内弁当	*Makunouchi Bentō*	With Vegetables, Fish Paste, etc.
すきやき弁当	*Sukiyaki Bentō*	With Sukiyaki
のり弁当	*Nori Bentō*	With Dried Seaweed, Fish Paste, etc.
かきあげ弁当	*Kakiage Bentō*	With Deep-Fried Vegetables etc.

●——TEMAKI 手 巻 [Temaki]

梅しそ巻	*Ume Shiso Maki*	With Pickled Plum And *Shiso*
しばづけ巻	*Shibazuke Maki*	With Purple Pickled Vegetable (Made From Cucumber, Aubergine, etc.)
たくあん巻	*Takuan Maki*	With Yellow Pickled Radish
納豆巻	*Nattō Maki*	With Fermented Bean Curd

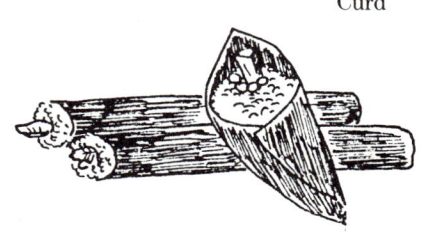

●——RICE BALLS　　おにぎり [Onigiri]

梅	Ume	With Pickled Plum
	(Umeboshi)	
鮭	Sake	With Salmon
おかか	Okaka	With Dried Bonito Shavings
たらこ	Tarako	With Cod's Eggs
天むす	Temmusu	With Deep-fried Shrimp

JAPANESE SYLLABARY ('*HIRAGANA*')

ひらがな

It is necessary to be able to read *Hiragana* for other types of menus, so now is a suitable time to introduce the *Hiragana* chart. The symbols are more distinctive than the corresponding *Katakana* and in this respect are easier to remember. However, from now on, you'll have to substantially increase your Japanese vocabulary.

あ	か	さ	た	な	は	ま	や	ら	わ	ん
a	ka	sa	ta	na	ha	ma	ya	ra	wa	n
い	き	し	ち	に	ひ	み		り		
i	ki	shi	chi	ni	hi	mi		ri		
う	く	す	つ	ぬ	ふ	む	ゆ	る		
u	ku	su	tsu	nu	fu	mu	yu	ru		

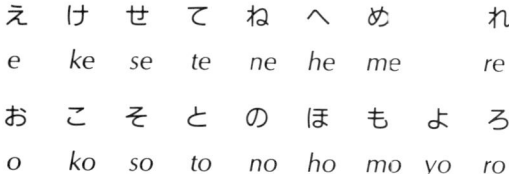

え	け	せ	て	ね	へ	め		れ
e	ke	se	te	ne	he	me		re
お	こ	そ	と	の	ほ	も	よ	ろ
o	ko	so	to	no	ho	mo	yo	ro

The pronunciation and rules which apply to *Katakana* are also true for *Hiragana* with the following exception. In *Hiragana*, the lengthening of the vowel is done by writing the appropriate vowel. Hence, *Mā* is written まあ although a long *Ō* is usually written using う (*U*). *Tō*, therefore, is とう .

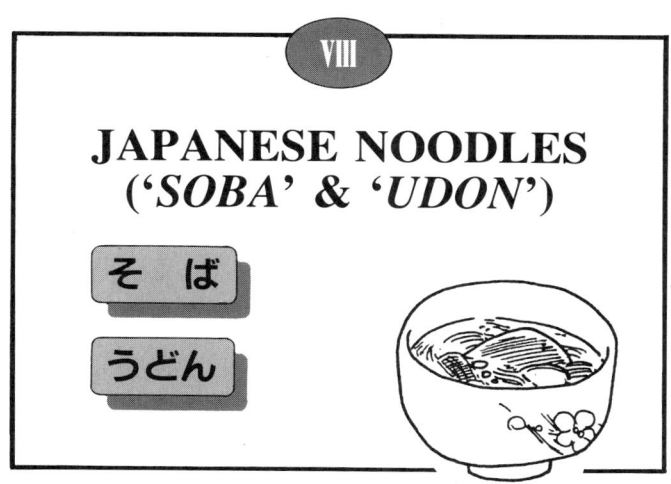

JAPANESE NOODLES ('*SOBA*' & '*UDON*')

そば

うどん

Cheap Japanese noodle restaurants (sometimes just stands) are popular with people in a hurry and can easily be recognized by そば *Soba* or うどん *Udon* written in *Hiragana* over the shop or printed on a red lantern hanging outside. *Soba* are 'Buckwheat Noodles' and *Udon* 'White Flour Noodles.' There is a choice of ingredients in addition to the basic noodles in soup and the plastic models displayed in the window give some indication of the food available. Some of the items listed below may only be available as either *Soba* or *Udon* — for example *Mori-soba* and *Nabeyaki-udon*.

●──NOODLES そば・うどん [Soba/Udon]

そ　ば	*Soba*	Buckwheat Noodles In Soup

41

うどん	*Udon*	White-flour Noodles In Soup
かけそば・うどん	*Kake-soba/-udon*	With Leek And Fish Paste (The Basic Noodle Dish)
きつね〜	*Kitsune-*	With Spring Onions And Fried Tofu
たぬき〜	*Tanuki-*	With Crispy Tempura Leftovers
月見〜	*Tsukimi-*	With Egg
山菜〜	*Sansai-*	With 'Wild Mountain Vegetables'
なめこ〜	*Nameko-*	With Tiny Yellow Mushrooms
おかめ〜	*Okame-*	With Fish Paste, Vegetables, etc.
カレー〜	*Karē-*	In A Curry-flavored Soup
肉南ばん〜	*Niku Namban-*	With Meat etc.
天ぷら〜	*Tempura-*	With Tempura
力〜	*Chikara-*	With *Mochi* (Compressed Rice)
鍋焼〜	*Nabeyaki-*	With Tempura, Egg, Vegetables, etc.
うどんすき	*Udon Suki*	Cooked At The Table 'Sukiyaki-style'
もりそば	*Mori-soba*	Cold Noodles Served With A Sauce
ざるそば	*Zaru-soba*	Similar To *Mori-soba* With Dried Seaweed on Top

天ざる	*Tenzaru*	*Zaru-soba* Served With Tempura
天せいろ	*Tenseiro*	A More Expensive version of *Tenzaru*
そうめん	*Sōmen*	Thin White Noodles Served Cold

These rice dishes are also normally available:

親子丼	*Oyako Don(buri)*	Chicken And Egg On Rice
カツ丼	*Katsu Don*	Pork Cutlet And Egg On Rice
他人丼	*Tanin Don(buri)*	Pork And Egg On Rice

▶▶ VOCABULARY ···

ざるそば [*Zaru-soba*] These *COLD BUCKWHEAT NOODLES*, served on a bamboo tray with dried seaweed on top, are dipped into a small dish containing a special sauce.

山 菜 [*Sansai*] Green and brown *MIXED WILD MOUNTAIN VEGETABLES*.

も ち [*Mochi*] This is *BOILED-AND-COM-PRESSED RICE*. It is eaten as part of *Osechi Ryōri* over the New Year's holiday but is also used in other types of cooking throughout the year.

鍋 [*Nabe*] This means *ONE-POT COOKING*. In this case, the tempura, egg and vegetables are cooked for a while together with the noodles.

丼 [*Don/Donburi*] This is meat, vegetables or egg *ON BOILED RICE WITH SOY SAUCE*. It is served in a large dish.

★ If you can't decide what to order and want to be a little adventurous, why not ask *Osusume wa nan desu ka?* (What do you recommend?)

★ You can express your approval of the food by saying *Oishii desu* (It tastes good) or *Daisuki desu* (I like it very much).

★ You are not likely to receive an *Oshibori* (A Wet Hand Towel) in the cheaper places but *Ocha* (Green Tea) is provided at no extra cost.

★ If you're afraid that they may have forgotten the *Sansai-soba* you ordered, say *Sansai-soba wa mada desu ka?*

IX

CHINESE FOOD

ラーメン

餃　子

中華料理

In addition to the numerous *Soba* and *Udon* shops, there are just as many serving cheap Chinese noodles (*Rāmen*), *Gyōza* and other popular Chinese dishes served with rice. Menus are often written in *Katakana* (even for the Japanese dishes) although *Hiragana* and *Kanji* frequently appear. The cheaper joints serve mainly noodles and have the *Katakana* for *Rāmen* (ラーメン) and *Kanji* for *Gyōza* (餃 子) clearly displayed, whereas if you see 中華料理 *Chūka Ryōri* (Chinese Cooking), there is likely to be a greater variety of dishes on the menu. The latter may have a selection of *Teishoku* (Set meals) available all day and at reasonable prices.

The list below includes the food in both the cheaper and more expensive Chinese restaurants. However, the 'up-market' places which offer an extensive selection with numerous specialties generally have the menu written in English, Chinese and Japanese.

●—NOODLES　　　ラーメン [Rāmen]

ラーメン	Rāmen	Chinese Noodles In Chicken Or Pork Broth
ワンタン	Wantan	*Wantan*
ワンタンメン	Wantanmen	*Wantan* With Noodles
チャーシューメン	Chāshūmen	Roast Pork With Noodles
ザーサイメン	Zāsaimen	Chinese Pickles With Noodles
タンメン	Tammen	Noodles With Fried Mixed Vegetables
みそラーメン	Miso Rāmen	Noodles In A Miso-flavored Soup
カレーラーメン	Karē Rāmen	Noodles In A Curry-flavored Soup
バターラーメン	Batā Rāmen	Noodles In A Miso-flavored Soup With Butter
塩ラーメン	Shio Rāmen	Noodles In a Salty Soup
スタミナラーメン	Sutamina Rāmen	'Healthy' Noodles With Liver, etc.
もやしそば	Moyashi Soba	Soup Noodles With Bean Sprouts
肉そば	Niku Soba	Soup Noodles With Meat
五目そば	Gomoku Soba	Noodles With Meat And Vegetables
チャンポン	Champon	Noodles Nagasaki-style
焼そば	Yaki Soba	Fried Noodles ('Chow Mein')
かたやきそば	Kata Yaki Soba	Crispy, Dried Fried Noodles

46

| ビーフン | Biifun | Thin Noodles |
| 冷し中華 | Hiyashi Chūka | Cold Noodles With Meat And Vegetables |

●—RICE   白　飯 [Hakuhan]

チャーハン	Chāhan	Fried Rice With Egg, Vegetables, etc.
五目チャーハン	Gomoku Chāhan	Special Fried Rice
カニチャーハン	Kani Chāhan	Fried Rice With Crab Meat
エビチャーハン	Ebi Chāhan	Fried Rice With Shrimps
中華丼	Chūka Don	Meat And Vegetables On Boiled Rice
天津丼	Tenshin Don	Crab Meat And Egg On Boiled Rice
白　飯	Hakuhan	Plain Boiled Rice

●MEAT & VEGETABLES   肉と野菜 [Niku to Yasai]

マーボードーフ（麻姿豆腐）	Mābō Dōfu	Bean Curd With Spicy Minced Meat
スブタ（酢豚）	Subuta	Sweet And Sour Pork
カニ玉	Kani Tama	Crab Meat With Scrambled Egg

春 巻	*Harumaki*	Spring Rolls
ギョーザ〔餃子〕	*Gyōza*	*Gyōza* (Minced Meat And Vegetables Fried In Dough)
シューマイ	*Shūmai*	Chinese Dumplings
八宝菜	*Happōsai*	Fried Meat And Vegetables In Sauce
野菜炒め	*Yasai Itame*	Quick-fried Green Vegetable
肉野菜炒め	*Niku Yasai Itame*	Quick-fried Meat And Vegetables
肉とキャベツの炒め	*Niku to Kyabetsu no Itame*	Quick-fried Meat And Cabbage
豚肉とピーマンの炒め	*Butaniku to Piiman no Itame*	Quick-fried Pork And Green Pepper
エビのチリソース煮	*Ebi no Chiri Sōsu Ni*	Shrimps In Chilli Sauce

●—SOUP　　　　　　　スープ [*Sūpu*]

野菜スープ	*Yasai Sūpu*	Vegetable Soup
玉子スープ	*Tamago Sūpu*	Egg Soup
コーンスープ	*Kōn Sūpu*	Corn Soup

●—OTHER FOOD

ザーサイ	*Zāsai*	Chinese Pickles
白 菜	*Hakusai*	White Cabbage
ナス〔茄子〕	*Nasu*	Aubergine (Eggplant)
ね ぎ	*Negi*	Spring Onions
きのこ	*Kinoko*	Mushrooms
パセリ	*Paseri*	Parsley
セロリ	*Serori*	Celery

レタス	*Retasu*	Lettuce
竹の子	*Takenoko*	Bamboo Shoots
鴨	*Kamo*	Duck
団 子	*Dango*	Small Dumpling
ピータン	*Piitan*	Preserved Eggs

▶▶ **VOCABULARY**·······························

チャーシュー | [*Chāshū*] *ROAST PORK CANTON-ESE-STYLE* cooked with soy sauce, sake, etc.

五 目 | [*Gomoku*] *MIXED*. (*lit.* Five Eyes)

チャンポン | [*Champon*] *NOODLES WITH FRIED VEGETABLES etc.* in a salty soup. This dish was originally from Nagasaki in Kyushu.

炒 め | [*Itame*] *QUICK-FRIED* or *FRIZZLED*. This is a common method of preparing Chinese food.

み そ | [*Miso*] *FERMENTED BEAN PASTE*. *Miso Shiru* (soup) accompanies most kinds of Japanese food and includes *Tōfu* and seaweed.

豆 腐 | [*Tōfu*] *BEAN CURD*. This is included in many types of Chinese and Japanese cooking and is considered quite healthy.

煮 | [*Ni*] *BOILED*. Although many types of food are boiled, this word suggests that the ingredients have been boiled together for a longer time than usual.

NOTE: The short words *to* (と) and *no* (の) mean 'and' and 'of' respectively.

49

●●• USEFUL LANGUAGE ·····························

★ If an English menu is available, you can easily order by pointing to your selection and saying *Kore kudasai* (This one, please).

★ As many dishes are written down as a long phrase, you can always use the above phrase or it is convenient to order by numbers if possible, adding the suffix -*ban* to the cardinal numbers listed in Chapter IV.

For example, *Jū-yon-ban o san-ninmae kudasai* can be translated as 'Three portions of number 14, please.'

Set meals are also generally numbered and can be ordered in the same way. If they are written as 'A', 'B' and 'C', just ask for 'A *Teishoku.*'

★ If you'd like some more tea, it's polite to say *Ocha itadakemasu ka?*. Note that *Ocha* can mean 'Chinese tea' or 'Japanese green tea.'

★ 'Chopsticks' in Japanese is *Ohashi, Osara* is a 'Plate' and *Ko Zara* is a 'Small Dish.'

★ You may need a fork or a spoon which are, naturally, *Fōku* and *Supūn.*

★ If the wrong dish is brought to your table or if the waiter misunderstands your order, simply say *Chigaimasu* (It is wrong), the meaning of which should be clear in this situation.

★ When ordering rice, you'll be asked when you want it brought (*Itsu odashi shimashōka?*). If you want it straight away, say *Saki ni. Ato de* means 'Later' and another phrase, *Issho ni* has the meaning of 'Together' or 'Served at the same time.'

★ There are usually set courses for 2 or more persons or you can leave the choice up to the restaurant by saying *Moriawase o kudasai* (Please bring a selection).

Moriawase 盛合せ also often appears on menus meaning a 'selection.' For example, 'A selection of fruit' is written: フルーツ盛合せ.

★ In some cheap eating places, it's necessary to purchase a ticket (食 券 *Shokken*) for your choice before you sit at the table.

★ *Nanji ni owarimasu ka?* means 'What time do you close?' and if you want to know the opening time, the phrase is *Kaiten wa nanji desu ka?*

X

SUSHI

す し　鮨

寿 司

Sushi comes in a variety of forms, the most typical being slices of raw fish etc. on top of vinegared rice and flavored with *Wasabi* (Japanese horseradish). They are usually served in pairs. The large conical-shaped pieces wrapped in dried seaweed (to make it easy to eat by hand) are called *Temaki* and the popular cylindrical variety are *Makizushi*. *Sashimi* (raw fish without the rice) may also be ordered. Rotating counters provide a convenient way of selecting your *Sushi* at some *Sushi-ya* or you can order a 'set' which is suitable for one or two persons. *Chirashi Zushi* (a selection of fish etc. served in a large dish on top of rice) is a substantial meal for one.

Many of the fish listed below may be ordered as both *Sushi* and *Sashimi*. Remember that the best *Sushi* is made with the freshest fish, so you should ask the proprietor for his recommendations.

Most *Sushi-ya* (also *Soba-ya*, *Rāmen-ya*, etc.) offer

Demae service. You place your order over the telephone and it is delivered to your door.

●──FISH 魚 [*Sakana*]

まぐろ	*Maguro*	Tuna
と ろ	*Toro*	Best Tuna (Pink)
はまち	*Hamachi*	Young Yellowtail
かんぱち	*Kampachi*	Similar To *Hamachi*
ぶ り	*Buri*	Yellowtail
さ ば	*Saba*	Mackerel
た い	*Tai*	Sea Bream
かつお	*Katsuo*	Bonito
いわし	*Iwashi*	Sardine
あ じ	*Aji*	Horse Mackerel
かれい	*Karei*	Turbot
すずき	*Suzuki*	Striped Bass
ひらめ	*Hirame*	Sole
かじき	*Kajiki*	Swordfish
え び	*Ebi*	Shrimp
甘えび	*Ama Ebi*	Sweet Shrimp
おどり	*Odori*	Live 'Dancing' Shrimps etc.
い か	*Ika*	Squid / Cuttlefish
た こ	*Tako*	Octopus
う に	*Uni*	Sea Urchin's Eggs
いくら	*Ikura*	Salmon Roe
かずのこ	*Kazunoko*	Herring Roe
とり貝	*Torigai*	Cockle
あおやぎ	*Aoyagi*	Round Clams
赤 貝	*Akagai*	Ark Shell
みる貝	*Mirugai*	Horse Clam
あわび	*Awabi*	Abalone

●━━SET DISHES

ちらし寿司	*Chirashi Zushi*	Fish etc. On Top Of Boiled Rice (Served In A Lacquer Dish)
特ちらし	*Toku Chirashi*	Special *Chirashi*
鉄火鮨	*Tekka Zushi*	*Sushi* With Tuna
にぎり鮨	*Nigiri Zushi*	Raw Fish On Rice
鉄火丼	*Tekka Don*	Raw Tuna On Rice
稲荷ずし	*Inari Zushi*	*Sushi* (With Rice) In Sweetened Deep-fried Bean Curd
江戸前ずし	*Edomae Zushi*	Special Selection Of *Sushi*

●━━TEMAKI　　　　　手 巻 [Temaki]

梅しそ巻	*Ume Shiso Maki*	With Plum And *Shiso* Leaf
いか納豆巻	*Ika Nattō Maki*	With Raw Squid And *Nattō*
たらこ巻	*Tarako Maki*	With Cod's Eggs
うに巻	*Uni Maki*	With Sea Urchin's Eggs
かっぱ巻	*Kappa Maki*	With Cucumber
しばづけ巻	*Shibazuke Maki*	With Pink Pickled Vegetable
たくあん巻	*Takuan Maki*	With Yellow Pickled Radish

●━━OTHER FOOD

玉子（卵）	*Tamago*	Egg (Usually Served As Sweet Omelette Topping)
明太子	*Mentaiko*	Spicy Fish Eggs

塩 辛	*Shiokara*	Squid's Inners
みそ汁	*Miso Shiru*	Miso Soup

▶▶ VOCABULARY ·····························

甘 | [*Ama/i*] *SWEET*. Also *Kara/i* means 'Hot' or 'Spicy.'
貝 | [*Kai/Gai*] *SHELLFISH*. Note that *Kai* becomes *Gai* at the end of a word.
納 豆 | [*Nattō*] *FERMENTED SOYBEANS*.
特 | [*Toku*] *SPECIAL*. The meaning is similar to *Jō* (上), although if both appear, *Toku* is more expensive.

●●● USEFUL LANGUAGE ·····················

★ You have a choice of sitting on the tatami floor (*Zashiki*), at a table (*Tēburu*) or the counter (*Kauntā*). *Zashiki ii desu ka?* means 'It is alright to sit on the *Zashiki*?'

★ In a *Sushi-ya*, the word for 'Tea' is *Agari* and it is served at the end of the meal in a large cup. Other 'Sushi-shop lingo' includes *Murasaki* (for *Shōyu* or 'Soy Sauce').

★ *Sushi* sets may be available as follows (in order of price):　梅　(*Ume*) — Plum
　　　　　　　　　　　　　竹　(*Take*) — Bamboo
　　　　　　　　　　　　　松　(*Matsu*) — Pine

These names may also be encountered in some other kinds of Japanese restaurants.

★ At lunchtime, after eating a set lunch, you may want to pay separately, so say, *Betsu betsu ni onegaishimasu.*

★ .....*mō (hitotsu)* means '(One) more ....'. In the same way, to ask for two more *Tokkuri* of hot sake, say *Atsukan mō nihon onegaishimasu.*

★ If you have enjoyed one dish and want to order the same again, just ask for *Onajimono.*

On walking into a restaurant, you are usually asked how many you are, and you can answer like this:

Hitori	1 Person
Futari	2 Persons
San-nin	3 Persons
Yo-nin	4 Persons

XI

JAPANESE CUISINE

日本料理

This section looks at the other types of food to be found in Japanese restaurants and includes some of the most characteristic dishes. Some restaurants specialize in one kind of cooking and others (especially the cheaper ones) might have a wide selection. In this chapter, there are descriptions of such typical 'Family Cuisine' as *Okonomiyaki* and *Kamameshi*, favorites such as *Tempura* and *Sukiyaki* right up to the exquisite (and expensive) *Kaiseki Ryōri* which every visitor to Japan should try at least once. Generally, Japanese food is simple, with any seasoning providing a subtle enhancement of the natural flavors and it is invariably beautifully presented.

●—YAKITORI　　　やきとり

Yakitori is grilled chicken on a stick and is best sampled in the *Akachōchin* (Red Lantern) establishments. Many parts of the chicken are used and a portion of *Yakitori* might include one stick each of chicken meat, skin, liver and heart. Ask for *Toriniku* if you only want the meat. You can choose to have it salted (*Shioyaki*) or with sauce (*Tare*). Order by the portion *(Ichi)-ninmae* or by the stick (using the counter *-hon*, see Chapter IV).

とり肉	*Toriniku*	Chicken Meat
つくね	*Tsukune*	Balls Of Minced Chicken
も　も	*Momo*	Leg
レバー	*Rebā*	Liver
ハ　ツ	*Hatsu*	Heart
手　羽	*Teba*	Wing
カ　ワ	*Kawa*	Skin
砂ぎも	*Sunagimo*	Gizzard
ささみ（梅）	*Sasami (Ume)*	Rare Chicken Breast With Pickled Plum
ささみ（明太子）	*Sasami (Mentaiko)*	Rare Chicken Breast With Spicy Fish Eggs

KUSHIYAKI & KUSHIAGE 串焼き・串揚げ

Yakitori is one type of *Kushiyaki*, that is small pieces of meat, seafood or vegetables grilled on a stick. The food is served on small individual dishes and often eaten with radish and soy sauce. Beef (牛 肉 *Gyūniku*) is a common meat used and typical vegetables include mushrooms (しいたけ *Shiitake*), green peppers (ピーマン *Pii-man*) and gingko nuts (ぎんなん *Ginnan*). Such combinations as 'Asparagus wrapped in bacon' (アスパラベーコン巻 *Asupara Bēkon Maki*) are prepared. Order by the stick (*Ippon, Nihon*, etc.) or ask for a selection (串焼き盛合せ *Kushiyaki Moriawase*) or a course (コース *Kōsu*) which may include raw stick vegetables as well.

For *Kushiage*, the food is deep-fried in breadcrumbs etc. and frequently *Shiso* or cheese, for example, might be added to produce a delicate variation on the basic meat and seafood. Some varieties are dipped into brown sauce in a small side dish.

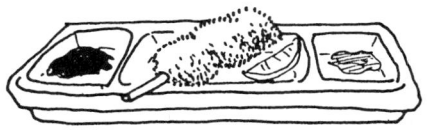

●—TONKATSU　　とんかつ

Tonkatsu means 'Pork Cutlet' and the meat is deep-fried in a mixture, including breadcrumbs. It is served with brown sauce and raw cabbage. This is hardly traditional Japanese food but its popularity has meant that it has developed into a distinctive style of cooking. The dishes may be ordered separately, but a *Teishoku* provides a substantial meal for one and is good value. In addition to the pork dishes, prawns and fish are often available. Here's a typical selection.

とんかつ定食	Tonkatsu Teishoku	Pork Cutlet Set
ロース定食	Rōsu Teishoku	'Tender' Pork Cutlet Set
ヒレカツ	Hire Katsu	Pork Fillet
串カツ	Kushi Katsu	Pork Cutlet And Onions On A Stick
メンチカツ	Menchi Katsu	'Minced Meat Cutlet'
エビフライ	Ebi Furai	Deep-fried Shrimps
あじフライ	Aji Furai	Deep-fried Horse Mackerel
きすフライ	Kisu Furai	Deep-fried Sillago
ミックスフライ	Mikkusu Furai	A Mixed Platter

●—TEMPURA　　天ぷら

Tempura is deep-fried prawns, fish and vegetables cooked in batter and dipped into *Tentsuyu* Sauce with radish. The best *Tempura* is served at places where the freshest ingredients and best quality oil is used. These restaurants which specialize in *Tempura* are rather expensive. In the cheaper shops where the oil is re-used (and often obtained from the expensive shops when they have finished with it), it can sometimes be a little uninspiring.

天ぷら定食	*Tempura Teishoku*	Tempura Set Meal
上天ぷら	*Jō Tempura*	Special Tempura
えび天	*Ebi Ten*	Prawn Tempura
天 丼	*Ten Don*	Tempura On Rice With Soy Sauce
天 重	*Ten Jū*	A More Expensive Version Of *Ten Don*

●—UNAGI   うなぎ

Eel is still a popular food, particularly amongst the older generation, and is best tried in the restaurants which serve mainly *Unagi* dishes. The slices of eel are charcoal-broiled in *Tare* sauce and there is a choice of different-sized portions. *Una Don* (うな丼), eel on rice with soy sauce or the more expensive *Una Jū* (うな重) in a special dish is suitable for one.

●──KAMAMESHI　　釜めし

Kamameshi is rice cooked together with meat, vegetables, etc., and served in a special pot. Here's a sample menu:

鳥めし	*Tori Meshi*	With Chicken
えびめし	*Ebi Meshi*	With Shrimps
かにめし	*Kani Meshi*	With Crab
鮭めし	*Sake Meshi*	With Salmon
うなぎめし	*Unagi Meshi*	With Eel
山菜めし	*Sansai Meshi*	With 'Wild Mountain Vegetables'
あわびめし	*Awabi Meshi*	With Abalone
たら子めし	*Tarako Meshi*	With Cod's Eggs
五目めし	*Gomoku Meshi*	Mixed

●──OKONOMIYAKI　　お好み焼

Okonomiyaki is a kind of pancake made with eggs and with pork, chicken, shrimps or vegetables, etc., and is cooked on a flat grill at the table. It takes practice to learn how to prepare it properly but the waitress will usually be happy to help you. It is quite a cheap way of eating and is especially popular with families.

牛　玉	Gyū Tama	With Beef
豚　玉	Buta Tama	With Pork
いか玉	Ika Tama	With Squid
えび玉	Ebi Tama	With Shrimps
ミックス玉	Mikkusu Tama	Mixed
野菜焼	Yasai Yaki	Fried Vegetables
焼そば	Yaki Soba	Fried Noodles

●──NABEMONO　　　鍋　物

Nabemono (One-pot Cooking) has been mentioned briefly earlier and is widely available in winter. A pot of water or stock is heated up in the middle of the table and, when it is boiling, the ingredients are added. It is cooked slowly and sometimes the food is dipped into some type of sauce before eating.

湯豆腐	Yu Dōfu	With Bean Curd
たらちり	Tara Chiri	With Cod (Usually Served With A Spicy Sauce)
かき鍋	Kaki Nabe	With Oysters
石狩鍋	Ishikari Nabe	With Salmon
寄せ鍋	Yose Nabe	Mixed

SUKIYAKI & SHABUSHABU   すきやき・しゃぶしゃぶ

Sukiyaki (すきやき) is probably the most internationally famous of all Japanese food, consisting of thin slices of beef, onions and other vegetables simmered in a sauce (with soy sauce and sweet sake) and dipped in beaten raw egg. It is cooked at the table in front of you. It is still considered an expensive dish and Japanese families are more likely to eat in at home than in a restaurant. *Shabu shabu* (しゃぶしゃぶ) is prepared by dipping the beef into boiling water for a few seconds. It is easy to order at these restaurants since the menu contains a choice of inclusive courses (コース *Kōsu*) and so it is only necessary to choose the course you want and to order your drinks.

KAISEKI RYŌRI   懐石料理

Kaiseki Ryōri establishments don't look like commercial restaurants (more like private houses) and you are likely to visit one when being invited or introduced by your Japanese host. *Kaiseki Ryōri* is traditionally eaten before the 'Tea Ceremony' and a course consists of perhaps as many as fifteen small dishes, each with a different character. The ingredients vary according to what is in season etc., but the meal will include a *Sashimi* dish, *Tempura*, *Nimono* (Boiled Things), *Yakimono* (Grilled or Baked Fish, for example), *Sunomono* (Vinegared Dish), *Agemono* (Deep-fried food), etc. At some point, you will be able to have the delicate *Chawammushi* which is a kind of egg-custard with small pieces of chicken, shrimp, mushroom or fishpaste.

All of these dishes are beautifully presented and, in contrast to other Japanese restaurants, the food is eaten in the order it is brought to your table. Although dishes may be ordered individually, it's really quite an experience to choose a course, although, as you might expect, these places are not cheap.

●—OTHER FOOD

Fish and *seafood* have long been the main diet in Japan, and besides being eaten raw, some varieties are typically marinated, broiled, baked, grilled and so on. However, the most common methods of cooking are *Shioyaki* (塩 焼), 'Salt-broiled' and *Kara-age* (唐 揚), 'Deep-fried.' Many of the fish listed in Chapter X may be prepared in these ways. Below is a further list of fish and seafood.

鮭	*Sake*	Salmon
にしん	*Nishin*	Herring
ま す	*Masu*	Trout
にじます	*Nijimasu*	Rainbow Trout
こ い	*Koi*	Carp
舌平目	*Shitabirame*	Sole
かます	*Kamasu*	Pike
あ ゆ	*Ayu*	Smelt
車エビ	*Kuruma Ebi*	Prawn
伊勢エビ	*Ise Ebi*	Lobster

Meat dishes are becoming increasingly popular, although they are mainly confined to chicken, beef and pork. In Western-style (洋 風 *Yōfū*) restaurants, however, it's possible to find veal (子牛肉 *Koushiniku*) and lamb (子羊肉 *Kohitsujiniku*). Also, in such places as beer gardens, *Jingisukan* ジンギスカン (marinated mutton) is occasionally available. The mutton and vegetables are grilled at the table and usually you can eat as much as you like for a fixed price within a certain time period.

In *Teppan' yaki* (鉄板焼) restaurants, the meat and vegetables are cooked by the chef on a grill in front of you. These kind of restaurants are becoming increasingly popular.

The adventurous might like to try *Fugu* (ふ ぐ) or 'Blowfish' which, since it is poisonous, is only available in certain licensed restaurants and in season (October to March). It is served in a variety of ways, for example as *Fugu Sashi* and *Fugu Chiri Nabe*.

Another interesting dish is the stew favored by sumo wrestlers, called *Chanko Nabe* (ちゃんこ鍋). This is a 'one-pot' (*Nabe*) dish containing a variety of fish, meat, vegetables and spices and, as can be imagined, it comes in large portions. You'll have to seek out the *Chanko Nabe* places since there are relatively few of them. Many of the owners are former sumo wrestlers themselves so you can expect the real thing.

Oden (おでん) consists of radish, seaweed, turnips, egg, etc., slowly simmered in stock. A few small restaurants specialize in this distinctive dish and it is served from a large simmering pot.

In *Bā*, *Sunakku* and *Pabu*, there may only be a limited selection of food available, but your drinks will be accompanied by either *Otsumami* (おつまみ), nuts, dried fish, etc., or *Tsukidashi* (つきだし) which are more substantial cocktail snacks.

XII

JAPANESE TEA HOUSES

甘味喫茶

In the big cities with numerous cafés, it's easy to overlook the traditional-style tea houses which, although often found in the quieter, more discreet locations, may also be sought out in such busy shopping streets as the Ginza in Tokyo. Whatever the location, they provide a calm, peaceful environment in which to relax. The decor is simple and you will be attended to by ladies in kimono. Sometimes you can hear koto or other traditional music.

You will be brought *Ocha* (ordinary green tea) when you first sit down and may then want to order another kind of tea, for example the thick, bitter *Matcha* which is the powdered tea used in the tea ceremony (*Ochakai*). This complements the very sweet cakes and desserts which are not to everyone's taste but should be tried.

Other attractively presented hot dishes are sometimes available, along with *Amazake* (甘 酒), a kind of thick, white, sweet sake, served warm. Together with the

Kaiseki Ryōri establishments, a visit to a tea house is recommended to the foreign visitor who would like a taste of old Japan.

●—TEA　　　　　　お 茶 [*Ocha*]

せん茶	*Sencha*	Ordinary Green Tea
麦 茶	*Mugicha*	Roasted Barley Tea
こぶ茶	*Kobucha*	Tea Made From A Type Of Seaweed
ほうじ茶	*Hōjicha*	A Roasted Brown Tea With A Rich Aroma
まっ茶（抹茶）	*Matcha*	Japanese Green Tea As Used In The Tea Ceremony
ウーロン茶（烏龍茶）	*Ūroncha*	Oolong Tea (Chinese Tea)

●—SWEETS 甘 味 [Kammi]

みつ豆	*Mitsumame*	Fruit In Syrup With Sweet Black Beans And Gelatine Cubes
クリームみつ豆	*Kuriimu Mitsumame*	*Mitsumame* With Vanilla Ice Cream
あんずみつ豆	*Anzu Mitsumame*	*Mitsumame* With Stewed Apricots
あんみつ	*Ammitsu*	*Mitsumame* With *Anko* (Very Sweet Bean Paste)
おしるこ	*Oshiruko*	Hot *Anko* Syrup With *Mochi*
ぜんざい	*Zenzai*	Hot Sweet Beans
ようかん	*Yōkan*	Sweet Bean Jelly
葛	*Kuzu*	Geletine-like Substance Made From Vegetable Extract
おはぎ	*Ohagi*	*Anko* With *Mochigome* (Rice) Inside
和菓子	*Wagashi*	A Typical Japanese Sweet
まんじゅう	*Manjū*	Steamed Bean-filled Dumplings
ところてん	*Tokoroten*	Traditional Dish With Seaweed Gelatine, Vinegar, etc.

●—CRUSHED ICE かき氷 [Kakigōri]

In this section, it's also worth mentioning other kinds of sweets which are popular in summer. *Kakigōri*

(かき氷) or *Furappe* (フラッペ) is crushed ice topped with syrup. Some of the most common types are listed here:

みぞれ	*Mizore*	With A White, Milky Syrup
イチゴ	*Ichigo*	With Strawberry Syrup
レモン	*Remon*	With Lemon Syrup
まっ茶(宇治)	*Matcha (Uji)*	With Green-Tea Flavored Syrup
宇治金時	*Ujikintoki*	With *Anko* And *Matcha*

XIII

'IZAKAYA' FARE
(including menu review)

居酒屋

An *Izakaya* is a cheapish drinking bar which usually offers a wide selection of Japanese, Western (and sometimes Chinese) dishes. The quality of the food varies from place to place and you should not expect the *Sashimi* to be as good as that as in a fine *Sushi* bar, for example. Below are the kind of dishes you can expect to find in *Izakaya* in addition to those available at other similar establishments (*Robatayaki* etc.). Many of the words should be familiar by now and this sample menu provides ample revision material in addition to the unique *Izakaya* fare.

●—DRINKS 飲み物 [*Nomimono*]

ビンビール	*Bin Biiru*	Bottled Beer
生ビール	*Nama Biiru*	Draught Beer
小ジョッキ	*Shō Jokki*	Small Glass ('Jockey')

中ジョッキ	Chū Jokki	Medium Glass
大ジョッキ	Dai Jokki	Large Glass
ライトビール	Raito Biiru	Light Beer
黒ビール（缶）	Kuro Biiru (Kan)	Black Beer (In A Can)
チューハイ	Chūhai	Chūhai (Shōchū With Soda)
レモンサワー	Remon Sawā	'Lemon Sour' (With Shōchū, Soda And Lemon Juice)
ライムサワー	Raimu Sawā	'Lime Sour'
梅サワー	Ume Sawā	'Plum Sour'
ウーロンサワー	Ūron Sawā	'Oolong Tea Sour'
グレープフルーツサワー	Gurēpufurūtsu Sawā	'Grapefruit Sour'
お 酒	Osake	Sake
日本酒	Nihonshu	Sake
焼 酎	Shōchū	Shōchū (A Cheap Liquor)
ウイスキー	Uisukii	Whiskey
水割り	Mizuwari	Whiskey With Water And Ice
オン・ザ・ロック	Onzarokku	'On The Rocks'
ハイボール	Haibōru	Highball
オールド	Ōrudo	'Old' Brand Whiskey
リザーブ	Rizābu	'Reserve' Brand Whiskey
スーパーニッカ	Sūpā Nikka	'Super Nikka' Brand Whiskey
氷	Kōri	Ice
お 湯	Oyu	Hot Water
ソーダ	Sōda	Soda
レモンスライス	Remon Suraisu	Slices Of Lemon
ワイン（白・赤）	Wain (Shiro/Aka)	Wine (White/Red)
ブルーハワイ	Burū Hawai	Blue Hawaii (Cocktail)
マルガリータ	Marugariita	Margerita
ソルティードッグ	Sorutii Doggu	Salty Dog
マイタイ	Maitai	Mai Tai
チ チ	Chichi	Chi Chi

スクリュードライバー	*Sukuryūdoraibā*	Screwdriver
ジントニック	*Jin Tonikku*	Gin And Tonic
シェリー	*Sherii*	Sherry
コーラ	*Kōra*	Cola
ジュース	*Jūsu*	Juice (=Any Kind Of Fruit Drink)
サイダー	*Saidā*	Cider (Non-alcoholic)
カルピス	*Karupisu*	'Calpis' (A Sweet, Milky Drink)

●──SMALL DISHES

もろキュー	*Morokyū*	Cucumber With Miso
梅キュー	*Umekyū*	Cucumber With Pickled Plum
枝豆	*Edamame*	Green Soybeans
お新香	*Oshinko*	Pickled Vegetables
漬物	*Tsukemono*	Pickled Vegetables
キムチ	*Kimuchi*	Pickled White Cabbage (Korean Style)
塩辛	*Shiokara*	Squid's Inners
かにみそ	*Kanimiso*	Crab's Eggs
梅たたき	*Ume Tataki*	Minced Sour Plum
なめこおろし	*Nameko Oroshi*	Small Mushrooms With Grated Radish (*Daikon*)
しらすおろし	*Shirasu Oroshi*	Baby Sardine With Grated Radish
コンニャク刺	*Konnyaku Sashi*	Uncooked *Konnyaku* (Made From Devil's Tongue Root Starch)
いなご	*Inago*	Seasoned Grasshoppers

●—VEGETABLE DISHES

コーンバター	Kōn Batā	Buttered Corn
えのきバター	Enoki Batā	Long White Mushrooms Cooked In Butter
ホウレン草バター	Hōrensō Batā	Buttered Spinach
なす焼	Nasu Yaki	Fried Aubergine
なす田楽	Nasu Dengaku	Aubergine Topped With Sweet Miso
おでん	Oden	Oden (Radish, Seaweed, Egg, etc., In Stock)
春 巻	Harumaki	Spring Rolls
さつまいも	Satsumaimo	Sweet Potato
山かけ	Yamakake	Mountain Potato
ししとう	Shishitō	Small Green Peppers
ピーマン	Piiman	Green Pepper
にんにく	Ninniku	Garlic
玉ねぎ	Tamanegi	Onion
オニオンスライス	Onion Suraisu	Onion Slices
長ねぎ	Naganegi	Spring Onions
しいたけ	Shiitake	Brown Mushrooms
おひたし	Ohitashi	Boiled Spinach With Dried Bonito Shavings And Soy Sauce

●—SALADS　　サラダ [Sarada]

グリーンサラダ	Guriin Sarada	Green Salad
トマトサラダ	Tomato Sarada	Tomato Salad
チキンサラダ	Chikin Sarada	Chicken Salad
シーフードサラダ	Shiifūdo Sarada	Seafood Salad
アスパラサラダ	Asupara Sarada	Asparagus Salad

カニサラダ	*Kani Sarada*	Crab Salad
コーンサラダ	*Kōn Sarada*	Corn Salad
豆腐サラダ	*Tōfu Sarada*	Bean Curd Salad
海草サラダ	*Kaisō Sarada*	Mixed Seaweed Salad
小えびサラダ	*Ko Ebi Sarada*	Shrimp Salad
ミックスサラダ	*Mikkusu Sarada*	Mixed Salad
ツナサラダ	*Tsuna Sarada*	Tuna Salad
和風サラダ	*Wafū Sarada*	Japanese-style Salad
中華風サラダ	*Chūkafū Sarada*	Chinese-style Salad
生野菜	*Nama Yasai*	Raw Vegetables (Salad)

●──POTATO DISHES ポテト [*Poteto*]

フライドポテト	*Furaido Poteto*	French Fries
ポテトフライ	*Poteto Furai*	French Fries
じゃがいもバター	*Jagaimo Batā*	Buttered Potato
肉じゃが	*Niku Jaga*	Potato And Meat Stew
ポテトチーズ揚げ	*Poteto Chiizu Age*	Deep-fried Potato With Cheese

●──BEAN CURD DISHES 豆 腐 [*Tōfu*]

冷 奴	*Hiyayakko*	Uncooked Tofu
湯豆腐	*Yu Dōfu*	Tofu Cooked In Boiling Water
豆腐のステーキ	*Tōfu no Sutēki*	Large Piece Of Fried Tofu ('Tofu Steak')
厚 揚	*Atsuage*	Deep-fried Tofu
肉豆腐	*Niku Dōfu*	Boiled Tofu And Meat Stew
揚出し豆腐	*Agedashi Dōfu*	Deep-fried Tofu In Stock

●──MEAT DISHES

肉 [Niku]

煮 込	Nikomi	A Stewed Meat Dish
スペアリブ	Supea Ribu	Spare Ribs
牛肉のたたき	Gyūniku no Tataki	Rare Beef (Served With Ginger)
牛ロース串焼	Gyū Rōsu Kushiyaki	Beef Grilled On A Skewer
ラムステーキ	Ramu Sutēki	Lamb 'Steak'
串カツ	Kushi Katsu	Skewered Deep-fried Pork With Onions
焼 豚	Yaki Buta	Roast Pork
ホルモン焼	Horumon Yaki	Grilled Liver etc.
牛もつ煮込	Gyū Motsu Nikomi	*Nikomi* With Liver etc.
牛レバー刺	Gyūrebā Sashi	Raw Ox Liver
馬 刺	Basashi	Raw Horse Meat
ポークソーセージ	Pōku Sōsēji	Pork Sausage
ラビオリ	Rabiori	Ravioli

"Dōmo .... dōmo .... dōmo ...."

生ハム	Nama Hamu	Raw Ham
くじらベーコン	Kujira Bēkon	Whale Bacon
豚柳川鍋	Buta Yanagawa Nabe	Pork And Egg Dish
すきやき鍋	Sukiyaki Nabe	'Sukiyaki-style' Dish
アスパラベーコン巻	Asupara Bēkon Maki	Asparagus Wrapped In Bacon
えのきベーコン巻	Enoki Bēkon Maki	Mushrooms Wrapped In Bacon
すずめ	Suzume	Grilled Sparrow (Usually *Kushiyaki*)

●CHICKEN DISHES 鳥 肉 [*Toriniku*]

やきとり（焼鳥）	Yakitori	Grilled Chicken On A Stick
つくね	Tsukune	Minced Chicken Balls
手羽先	Tebasaki	Chicken Wings
とりの唐揚	Tori no Kara-age	Crispy Deep-fried Chicken
若どりの唐揚	Wakadori no Kara-age	Crispy Deep-fried Young Chicken

●RAW FISH 刺 身 [*Sashimi*]

まぐろ	Maguro	Tuna
はまち	Hamachi	Young Yellowtail
い　か	Ika	Squid
た　こ	Tako	Octopus
まぐろぶつ	Maguro Butsu	'Hacked' Pieces Of Raw Tuna
たこぶつ	Tako Butsu	Pieces Of Raw Octopus
甘えび	Ama Ebi	Sweet Shrimp

あわび	Awabi	Abalone
かつおのたたき	Katsuo no Tataki	Bonito
あじのたたき	Aji no Tataki	Horse Mackerel
刺身盛合せ	Sashimi Moriawase	A Selection Of *Sashimi*
七 品	Nanahin	Seven Kinds

●— OTHER FISH & SEAFOOD DISHES シーフード [Shiifūdo]

ししゃも	Shishamo	Small Fish (Grilled)
焼さば	Yaki Saba	Grilled Mackerel
焼さんま	Yaki Samma	Grilled Mackerel Pike
ほっけ	Hokke	Fish From Northern Japan
にしん	Nishin	Herring
どじょうの唐揚	Dojō no Kara-age	Deep-fried Loach
かれいの唐揚	Karei no Kara-age	Deep-fried Turbot
ほたて貝	Hotate Gai	Scallops
あさりバター	Asari Batā	Short-necked Clams In Butter

あさりの酒蒸し	*Asari no Sakemushi*	Short-necked Clams In Sake
たこ焼	*Tako Yaki*	Wheat-flour Dumpling With Bits Of Octopus, Ginger, Cabbage, etc.
いか納豆	*Ika Nattō*	Raw Squid With *Nattō*
まぐろ納豆	*Maguro Nattō*	Raw Tuna With *Nattō*
いか丸焼	*Ika Maruyaki*	Broiled Squid (Whole)
川えびの唐揚	*Kawa Ebi no Kara-age*	Small Shrimps, Deep Fried
げその唐揚	*Geso no Kara-age*	Deep-fried Squid's Tentacles
えびの塩焼	*Ebi no Shioyaki*	Prawn Grilled With Salt
しらうおの唐揚	*Shirauo no Kara-age*	Deep-fried Whitebait
柳川鍋	*Yanagawa Nabe*	Loach In A Thin Omelette
うな玉	*Unatama*	Eel And Egg
カニクリームコロッケ	*Kani Kuriimu Korokke*	Crab Cream Croquette
カニ甲羅揚	*Kani Kōra-age*	Deep-fried Crab Cream Croquette (Served In Shell)
はんぺん	*Hampen*	Fish Paste
ちくわ	*Chikuwa*	'Fish Sausage'
カキフライ	*Kaki Furai*	Fried Oysters
生ガキ	*Nama Gaki*	Raw Oysters
明太子	*Mentaiko*	Spicy Fish Eggs
さざえ	*Sazae*	Top Shell
えいひれ	*Eihire*	Dried Fins

● VINEGARED DISHES 酢の物 [*Sunomono*]

わかめ酢	*Wakame Su*	With Seaweed
くらげ酢	*Kurage Su*	With Jellyfish

もずく酢	*Mozuku Su*	With Fresh Seaweed
たこ酢	*Tako Su*	With Octopus
かに酢	*Kani Su*	With Crab
なまこ酢	*Namako Su*	With Sea Cucumber
メさば	*Shime Saba*	With Mackerel
酢の物盛合せ	*Sunomono Moriawase*	Mixed *Sunomono*
ねぎぬた	*Negi Nuta*	Spring Onions In Vinegar And Miso
わかめぬた	*Wakame Nuta*	Seaweed In Vinegar And Miso
まぐろぬた	*Maguro Nuta*	Raw Tuna In Vinegar And Miso
いかぬた	*Ika Nuta*	Raw Squid In Vinegar And Miso

●ONE-POT COOKING　　鍋 物 [*Nabemono*]

たらちり	*Tara Chiri*	With Cod (Usually Served With A Spicy Sauce)
かき鍋	*Kaki Nabe*	With Oysters
石狩鍋	*Ishikari Nabe*	With Salmon
寄せ鍋	*Yose Nabe*	Mixed

●RICE DISHES　　ごはん [*Gohan*]

おにぎり	*Onigiri*	Rice Balls
焼おにぎり	*Yaki Onigiri*	Broiled Rice Balls
ぞうすい	*Zōsui*	Rice Gruel
お茶漬け	*Ocha Zuke*	Rice In Green Tea
（鮭 のり 梅）	*(Sake/Nori/Ume)*	(With Salmon/Seaweed/ Plum)
ごはん	*Gohan*	Boiled Rice

81

●──SOUP 汁 物 [Shirumono]

みそ汁	*Miso Shiru*	Miso Soup
なめこ汁	*Nameko Shiru*	Soup With Mushrooms

●──NOODLES そば・うどん [Soba/Udon]

焼そば	*Yaki Soba*	Fried Noodles (Actually Chinese Noodles, not *Soba*)
焼うどん	*Yaki Udon*	Fried Noodles (*Udon*)

●──DESSERTS デザート [Dezāto]

アイスクリーム	*Aisu Kuriimu*	Ice Cream
フルーツ盛合せ	*Furūtsu Moriawase*	A Selection Of Fresh Fruit
シャーベット	*Shābetto*	Sorbet

▶▶ **VOCABULARY**··

たたき | [*Tataki*] Literally, it means 'beaten' but may be translated as *SLICED* or *CHOPPED*. It is typically used for raw fish but may also refer to *RARE* meat or *MINCED* plum, for example. Additionally, *Tataki* emphasizes that the ingredients used are fresh.

揚 | [*Age*] *DEEP-FRIED. Kara-age* means that the oil has completely drained before serving, leaving the food dry and crispy.

ぶ つ | [*Butsu*] These are the *PIECES OF RAW FISH* that are left over after *Sashimi* has been prepared from the best part.

XIV

VOCABULARY SUMMARY
(Basic menu items excluding '*Katakana*' words taken directly from English ,etc)

SOME ADDITIONAL KANJI ARE INCLUDED

A ●
揚 (げ)	*Age*	Deep-fried........*58, 65, 76, 82**
あ じ	*Aji*	Horse Mackerel........*53, 60, 79*
赤 貝	*Akagai*	Ark-shell...........................*53*
甘 (い)	*Ama(i)*	Sweet....................*53, 55*, 78*
甘 酒	*Amazake*	Sweet Sake......................*68*
あんこ	*Ammitsu*	Fruit Syrup With *Anko* *69*
あんみつ	*Anko*	Sweet Bean Paste................*70*
あんず	*Anzu*	Apricot............................*70*
あおやぎ	*Aoyagi*	Round Clams.....................*53*
あさり	*Asari*	Short-necked Clams *80*
厚 揚	*Atsuage*	Deep-fried Bean Curd *62, 76*
あわび	*Awabi*	Abalone.....................*53, 79*
あ ゆ	*Ayu*	Smelt *66*

B ●
| 馬 刺 | *Basashi* | Raw Horse Meat ....*77* |

83

K ●

T ●

(""*"" indicates the page on which the menu item is explained in detail.)

91

OTHER USEFUL WORDS ●────────

食事	Shokuji	Meal
朝食	Chōshoku	Breakfast
昼食	Chūshoku	Lunch
夕食	Yūshoku	Dinner
おせち料理	Osechi Ryōri	New Year's Food

大根	Daikon	Large White Radish
かぼちゃ	Kabocha	Pumpkin
ニラ	Nira	Leek
人参	Ninjin	Carrot
れんこん	Renkon	Lotus Root
カリフラワー	Karifurawā	Cauliflower
ブロッコリー	Burokkorii	Broccoli
オリーブ	Oriibu	Olives
アンチョビー	Anchobii	Anchovies

果物	Kudamono	Fruit
梨	Nashi	Japanese Pear
桃	Momo	Peach
柿	Kaki	Persimmon
西瓜	Suika	Watermelon
みかん	Mikan	Tangerine
ぶどう	Budō	Grapes
さくらんぼ	Sakurambo	Cherries
パイナップル	Painappuru	Pineapple

米	Kome	Rice
麦	Mugi	Wheat/Barley

大 豆	*Daizu*	Soy Beans
レンズ豆	*Renzumame*	Lentils
小 豆	*Azuki*	Red Beans
からし	*Karashi*	Mustard
クッキー	*Kukkii*	Biscuits
せんべい	*Sembei*	Round Rice Crackers
あられ	*Arare*	Small Rice Crackers
ブランデー	*Burandē*	Brandy
ウオッカ	*Uokka*	Vodka
ラ ム	*Ramu*	Rum
コック	*Kokku*	Cook
ウエーター	*Uētā*	Waiter
ウエートレス	*Uētoresu*	Waitress
食べる	*Taberu*	To Eat
飲 む	*Nomu*	To Drink
灰 皿	*Haizara*	Ashtray
ナプキン	*Napukin*	Serviette

SIGNS

SIGNS INSIDE RESTAURANTS——

営業中	*Eigyōchū*	**Open**
休業中	*Kyūgyōchū*	**Closed**
準備中	*Jumbichū*	**Opening/Closing Soon**
お手洗	*Otearai*	**Toilet**
男	*Otoko*	**Men**
女	*Onna*	**Women**
入　口	*Iriguchi*	**Entrance**
出　口	*Deguchi*	**Exit**
非常口	*Hijōguchi*	**Emergency Exit**
押（す）	*Osu*	**Push**
引（く）	*Hiku*	**Pull**
塩	*Shio*	**Salt**
コショウ	*Koshō*	**Pepper**
酢	*Su*	**Vinegar**
しょうゆ	*Shōyu*	**Soy Sauce**
ソース	*Sōsu*	**Brown Sauce**

七味	Shichimi	Mixed Seasoning
砂糖	Satō	Sugar
本日のおすすめ	Honjitsu no Osusume	Special Dishes Today

SIGNS OUTSIDE IDENTIFYING RESTAURANTS

● **Restaurants**

焼肉	Yakiniku	Korean Barbecue
ファミリーレストラン	Famirii Resutoran	Family Restaurant
イタリア料理	Itaria Ryōri	Italian Food
ドイツ料理	Doitsu Ryōri	German Food
インド料理	Indo Ryōri	Indian Food
＊菜食レストラン	Saishoku Resutoran	Vegetarian Restaurant
＊西洋料理	Seiyō Ryōri	Western Food

● **Fast-Food**

ハンバーガー	Hambāgā	Hamburgers
サンドイッチ	Sandoitchi	Sandwiches
おべんとう／弁当	(O)bentō	Boxed Lunches

● **Chinese Food**

中華料理	Chūka Ryōri	Chinese Food
ラーメン	Rāmen	Cheap Chinese Noodles
餃子	Gyōza	Gyōza (Pot Stickers)

● **Japanese Cuisine**

日本料理	Nihon Ryōri	Japanese Food
和食	Washoku	Japanese Food
そば	Soba	Buckwheat Noodles

うどん	*Udon*	**White Flour Noodles**
すし／鮨／寿司	*Sushi*	*Sushi*
やきとり	*Yakitori*	**Skewered Chicken**
串焼き	*Kushiyaki*	**Skewered Meat etc. (Grilled)**
串揚げ	*Kushiage*	**Skewered Meat etc. (Deep-fried)**
とんかつ	*Tonkatsu*	**Pork Cutlet**
天ぷら	*Tempura*	**Tempura**
うなぎ	*Unagi*	**Eel**
釜めし	*Kamameshi*	*Kamameshi*
お好み焼	*Okonomiyaki*	**A Kind Of Pancake**
鍋物	*Nabemono*	**One-pot Cooking**
すきやき	*Sukiyaki*	**Sukiyaki**
しゃぶしゃぶ	*Shabushabu*	*Shabushabu*
懐石料理	*Kaiseki Ryōri*	**Formal Japanese Cuisine**
鉄板焼	*Teppan'yaki*	**Hot Plate Cooking**
おでん	*Oden*	*Oden*
＊料理屋	*Ryōriya*	**Traditional Restaurant**
＊小料理	*Koryōri*	**Small *Ryōriya***
＊炉ばた焼	*Robatayaki*	**Hearth Cooking**

●Cafés / Tea Houses

喫茶店	*Kissaten*	**Tea & Coffee Shop**
コーヒー店	*Kōhiiten*	**Coffee Shop**
コーヒーショップ	*Kōhii Shoppu*	**Coffee Shop**
甘味喫茶	*Kammi Kissa*	**Traditional Tea House**

●Drinking Bar

居酒屋	*Izakaya*	**Drinking Bar**
＊バー	*Bā*	**Bar**
＊パブ	*Pabu*	**Pub**
＊スナック	*Sunakku*	**Small Drinking Bar**
＊ビヤガーデン	*Biya Gāden*	**Beer Garden**